Presenting:

THINK PINK

GET IN SYNC WITH THE COLOR PINK!

WORDS & ART BY: BRIANNA DAVIS

I0433321

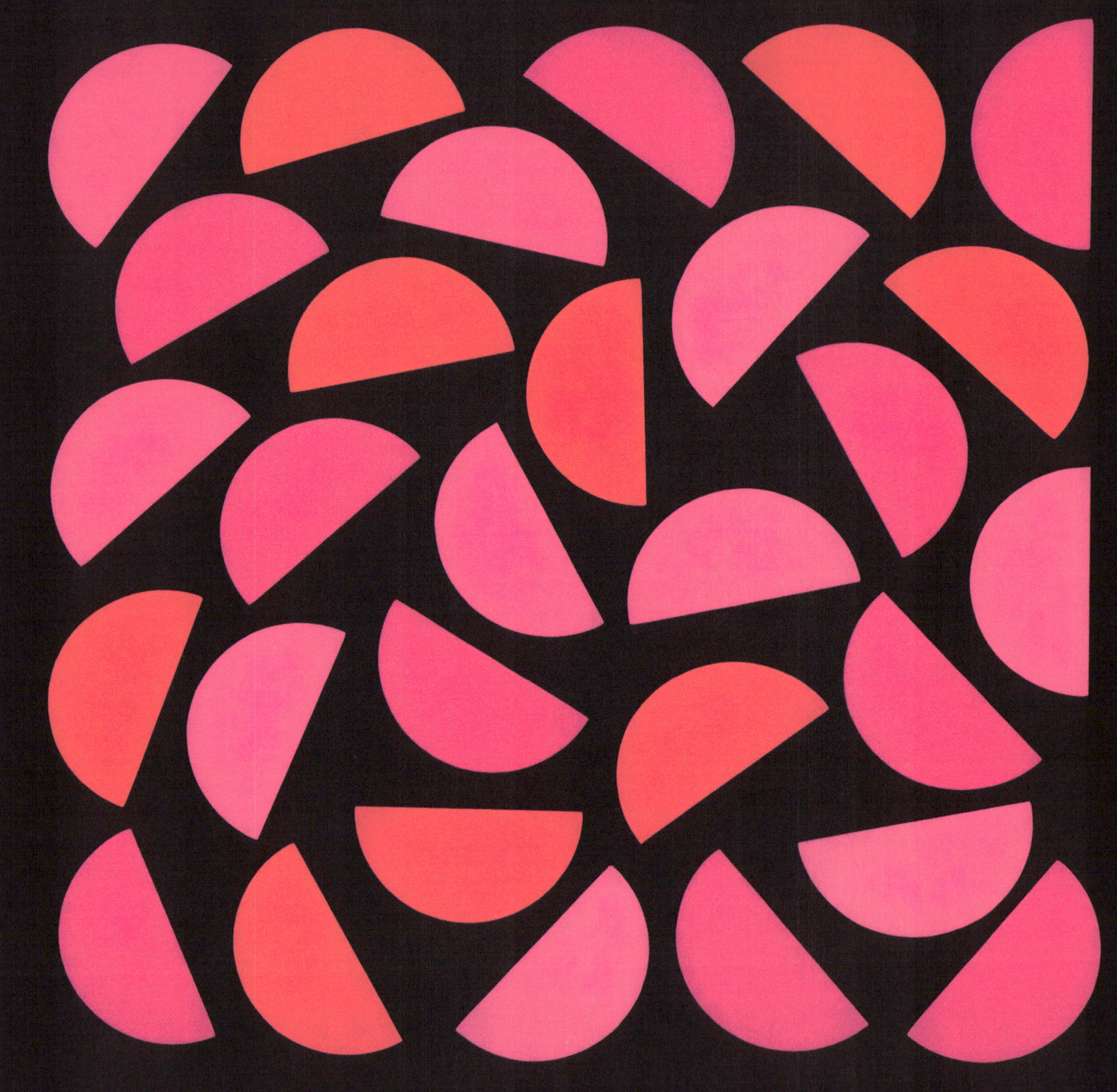

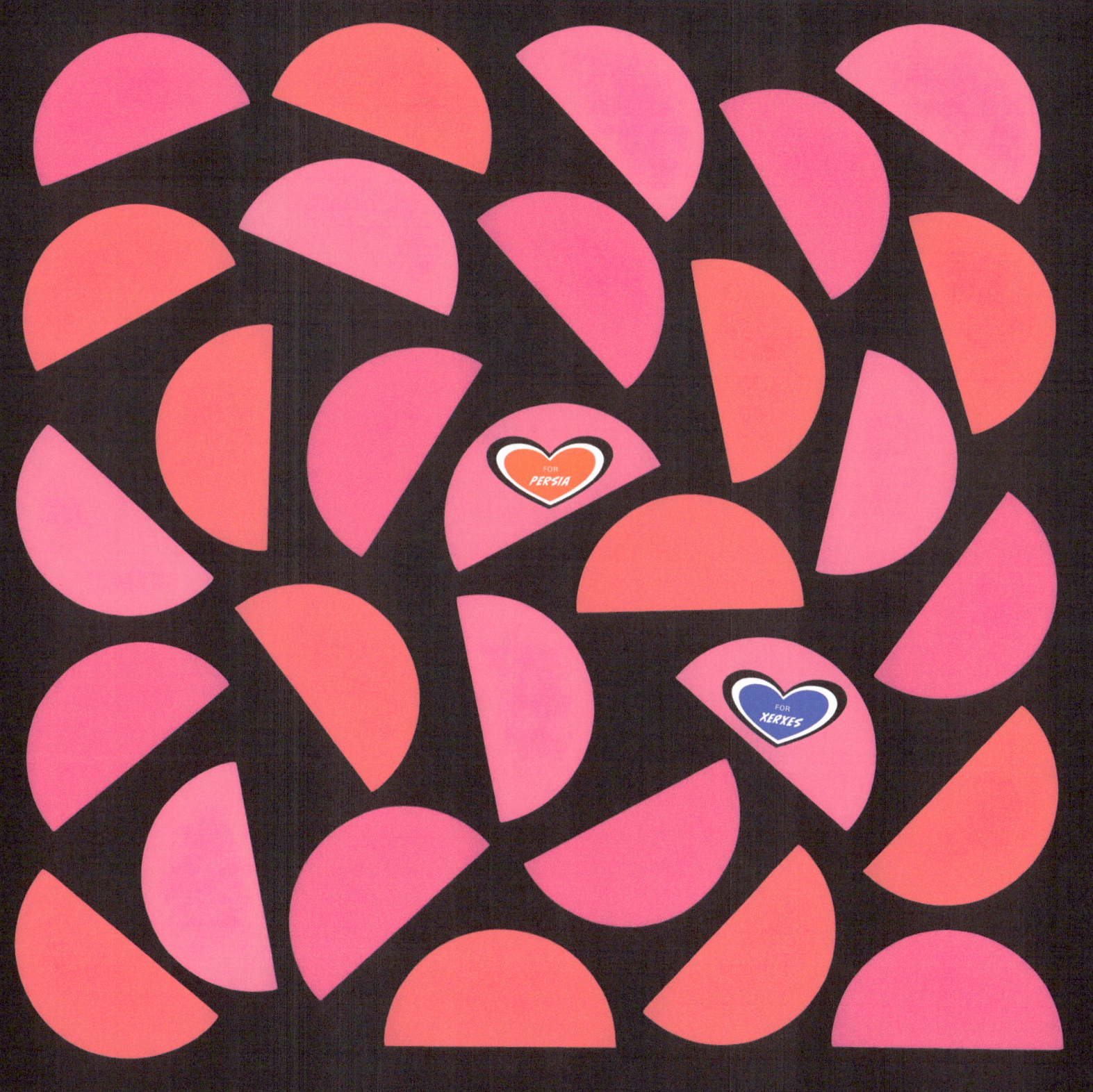

PINK

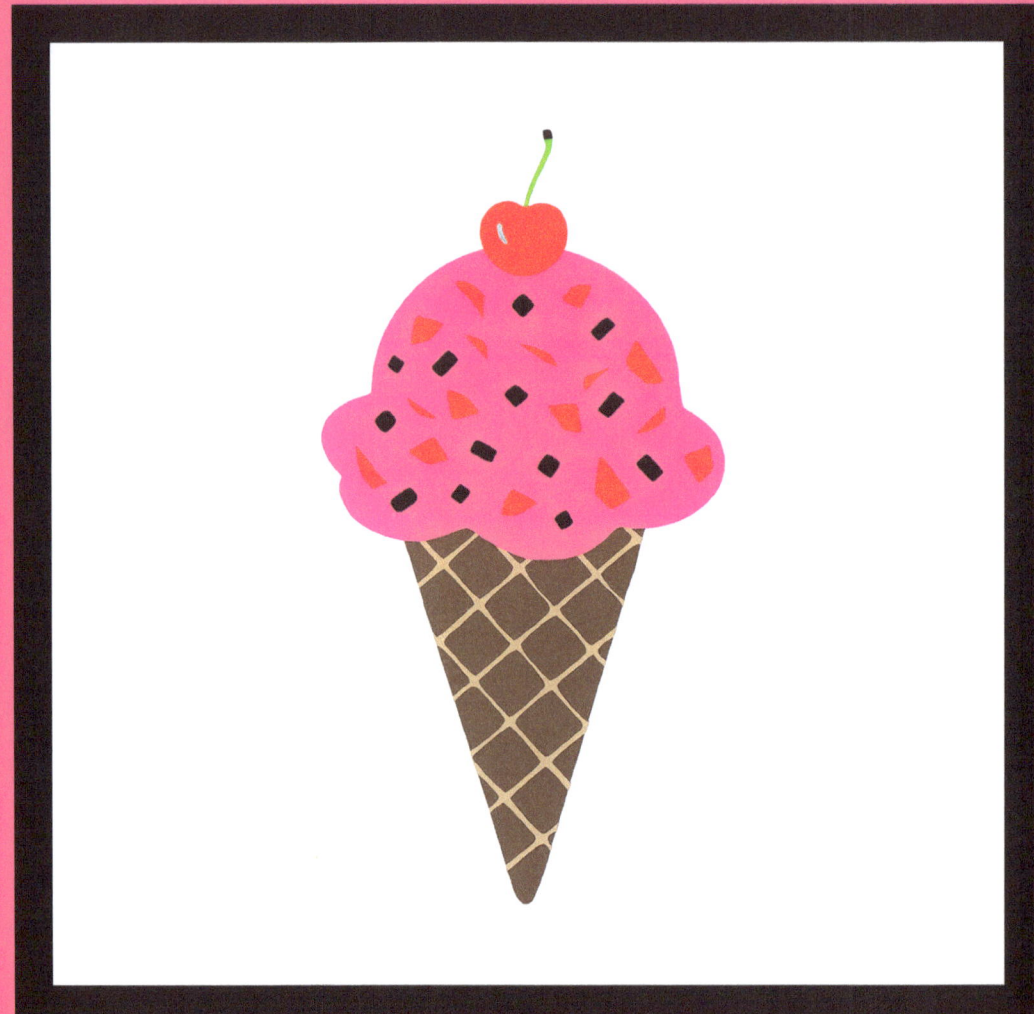

CHERRY CHIP ICE CREAM IS A NICE SUMMER SWEET...

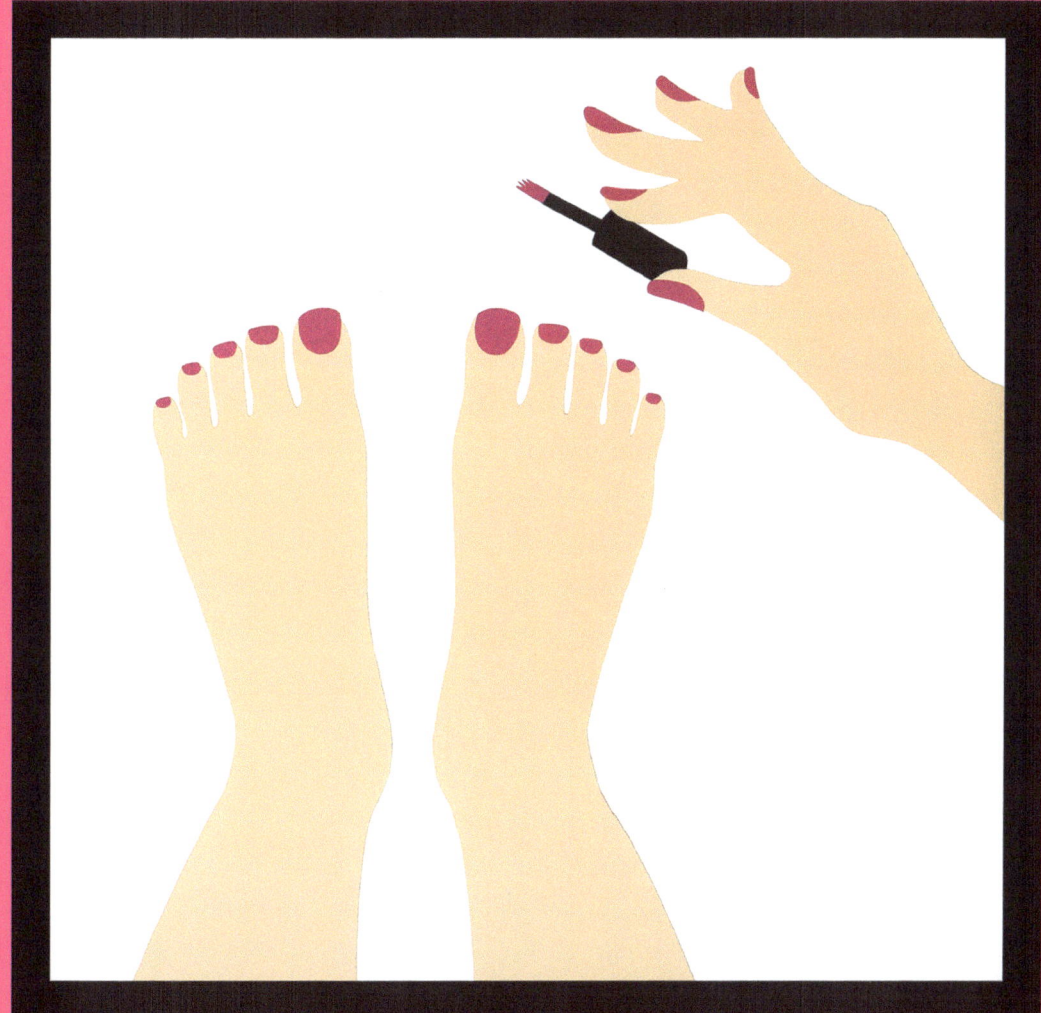

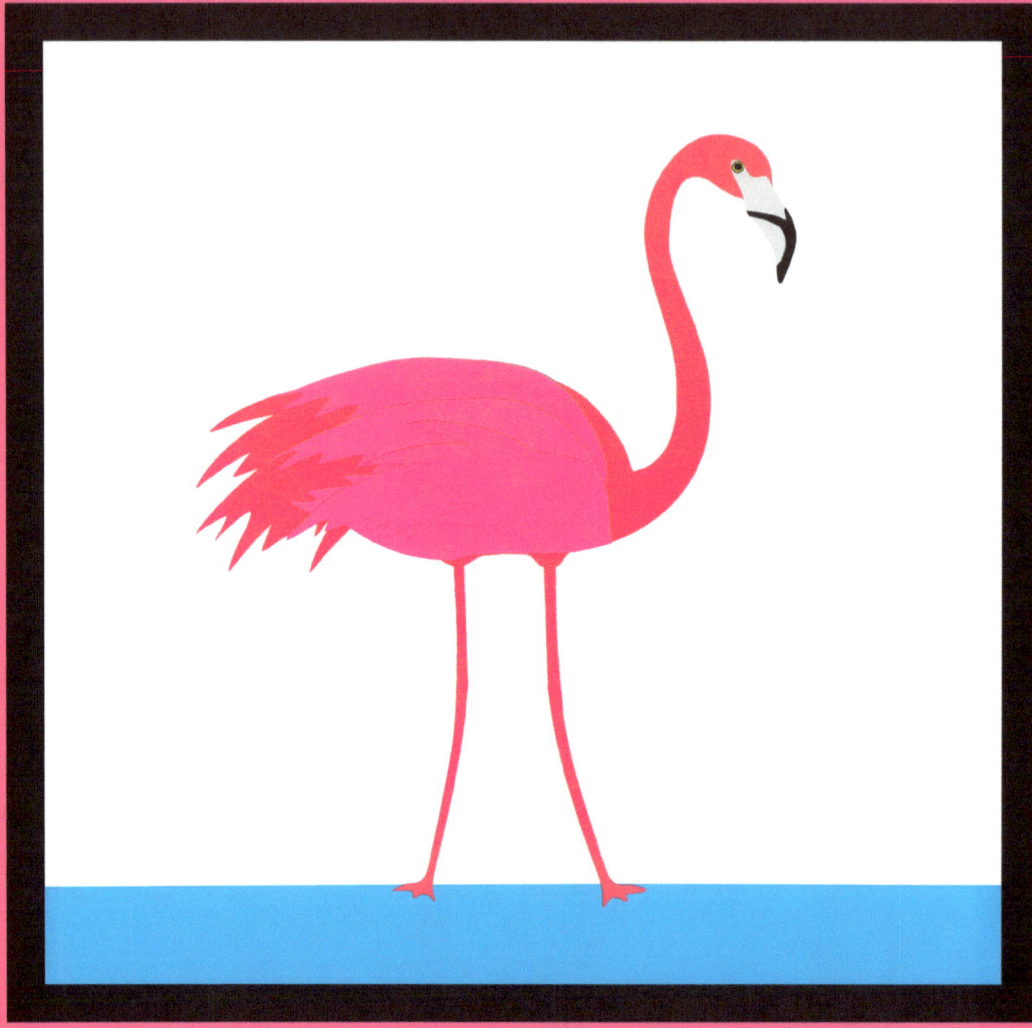

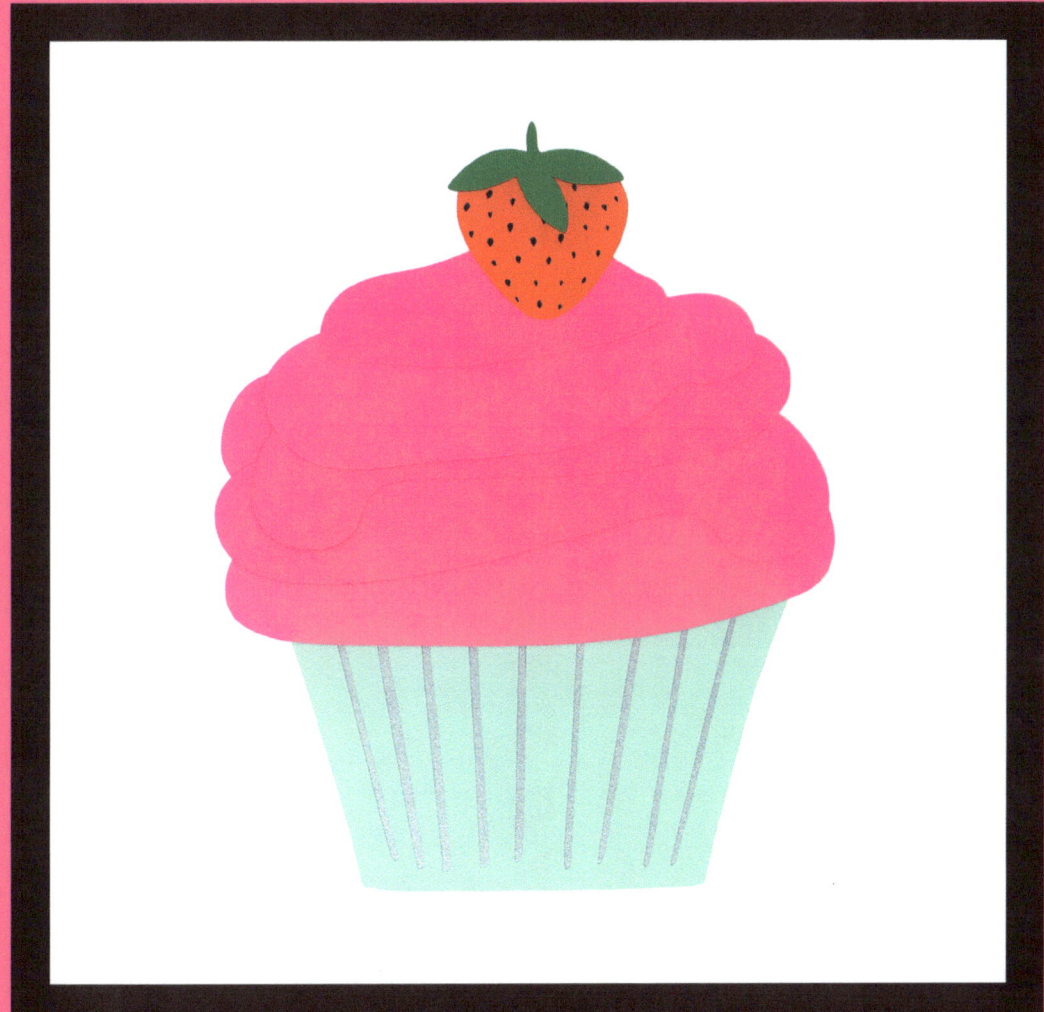

AT A PARTY, A STRAWBERRY CUPCAKE IS A DELICIOUS TREAT!

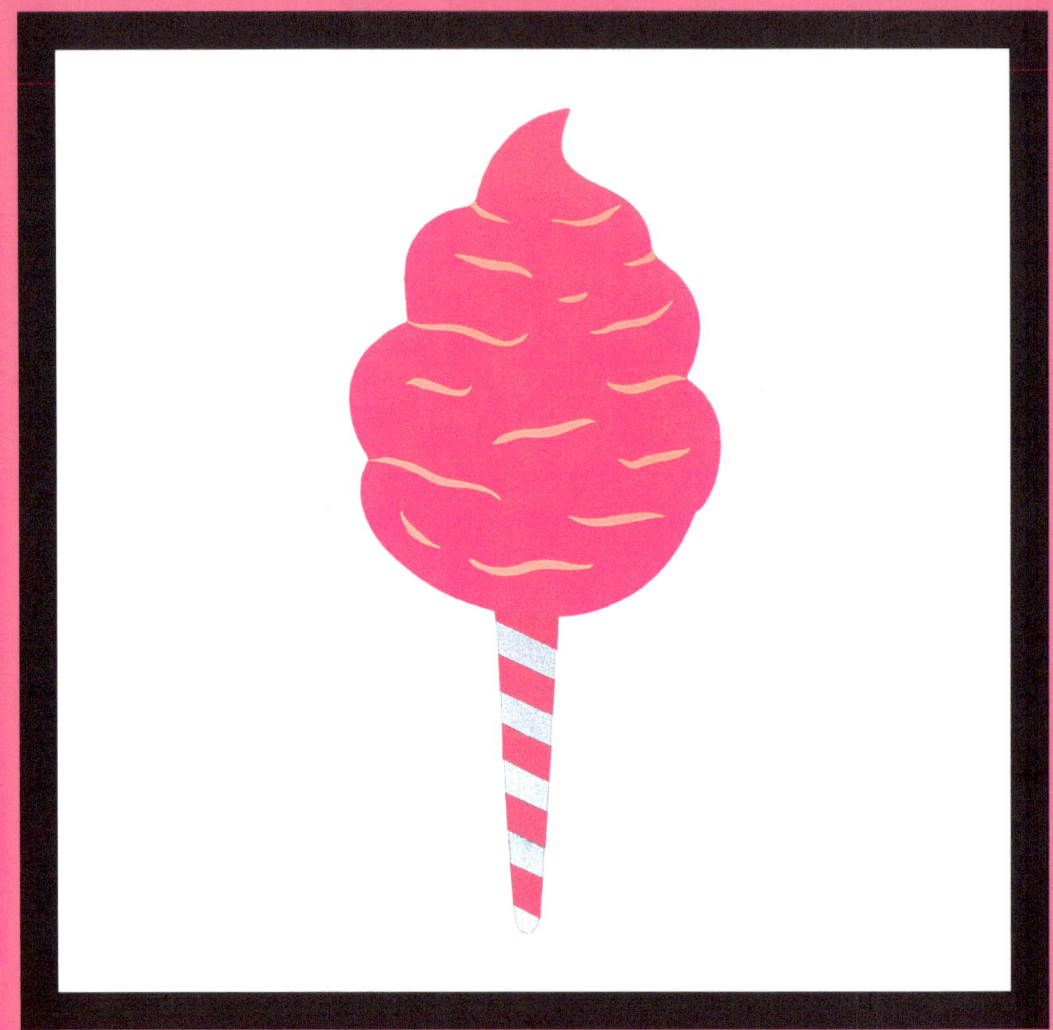

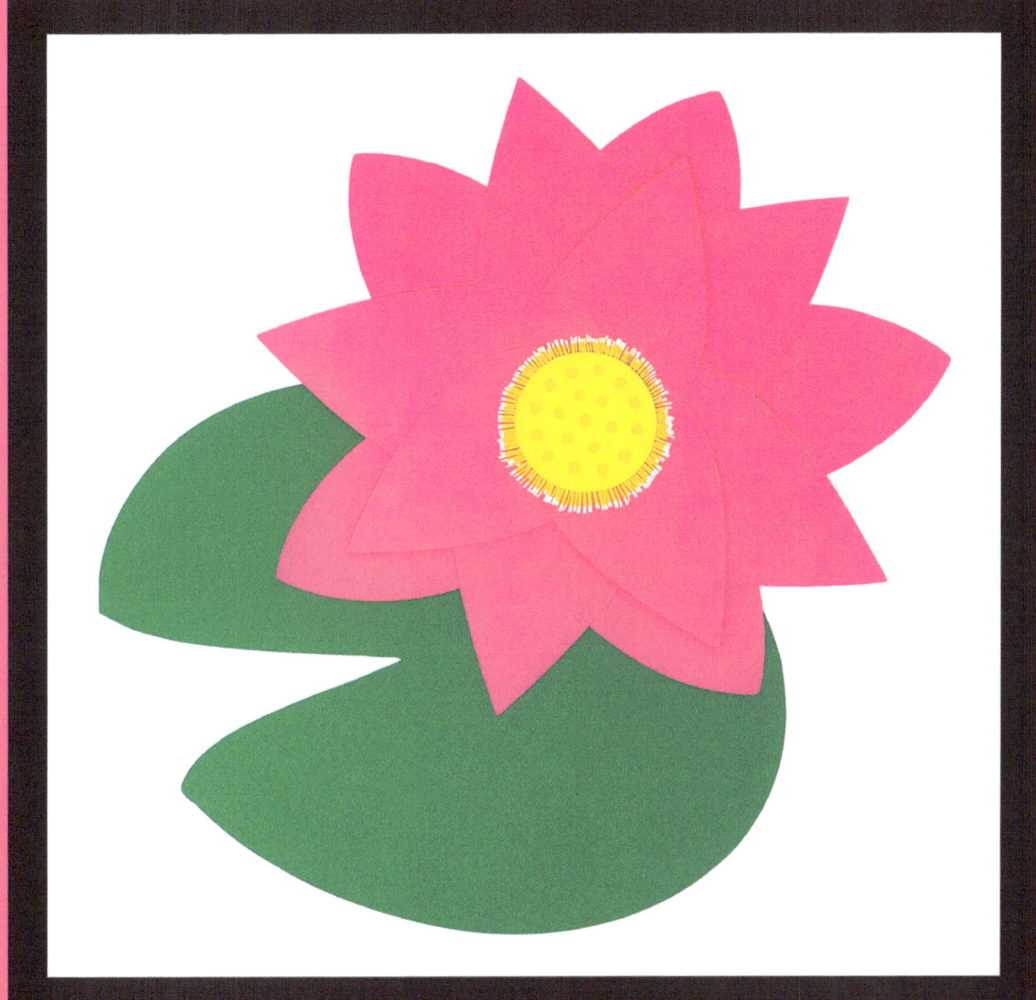

IN THE MORNING, THE PINK LOTUS GETS FULLER!

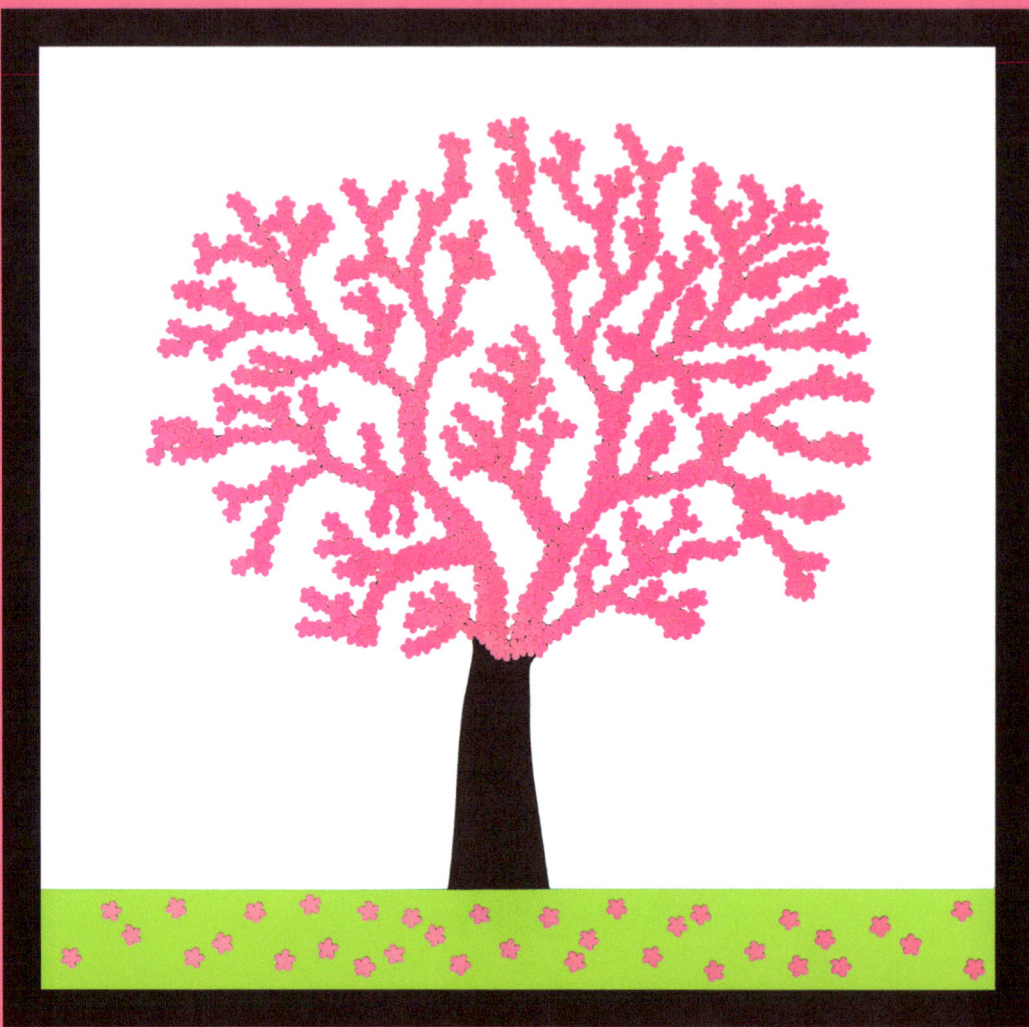

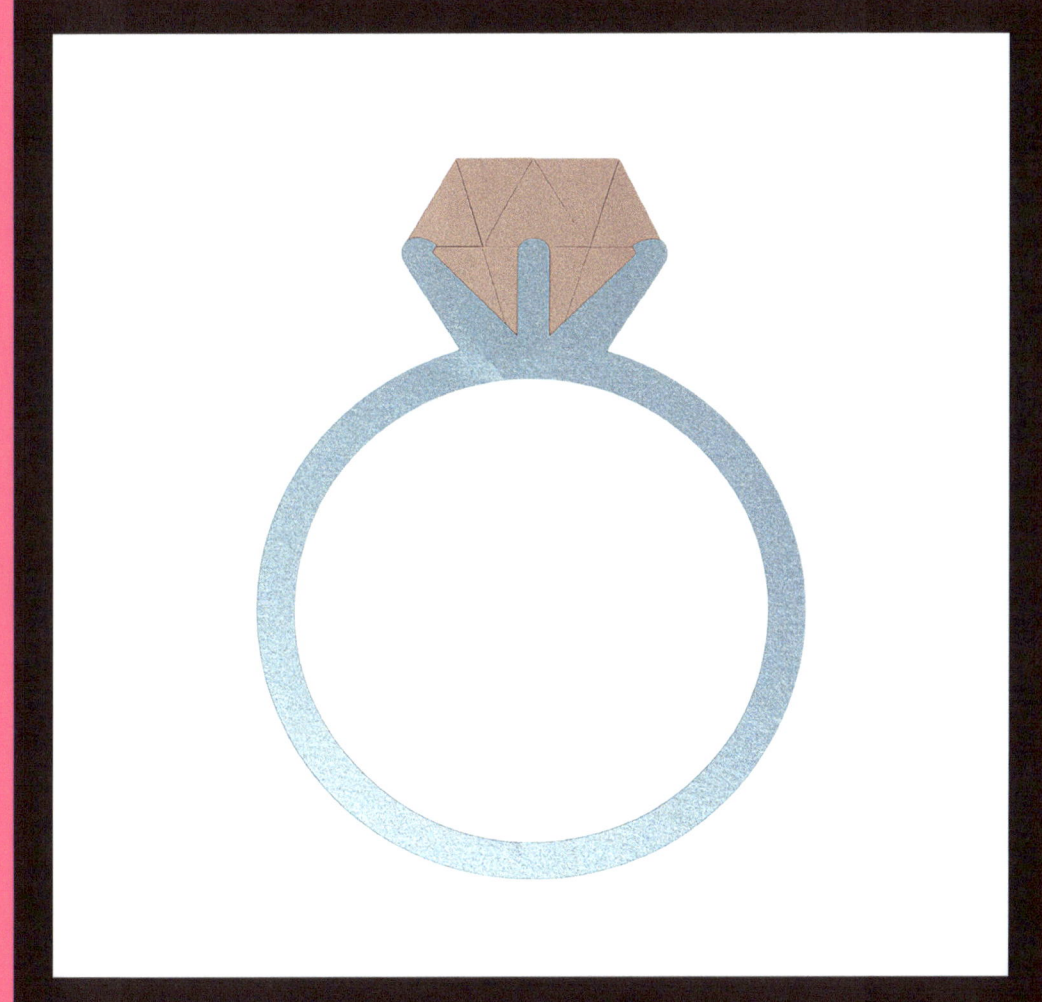

ROSE QUARTZ IS A POPULAR STONE FOR A RING!

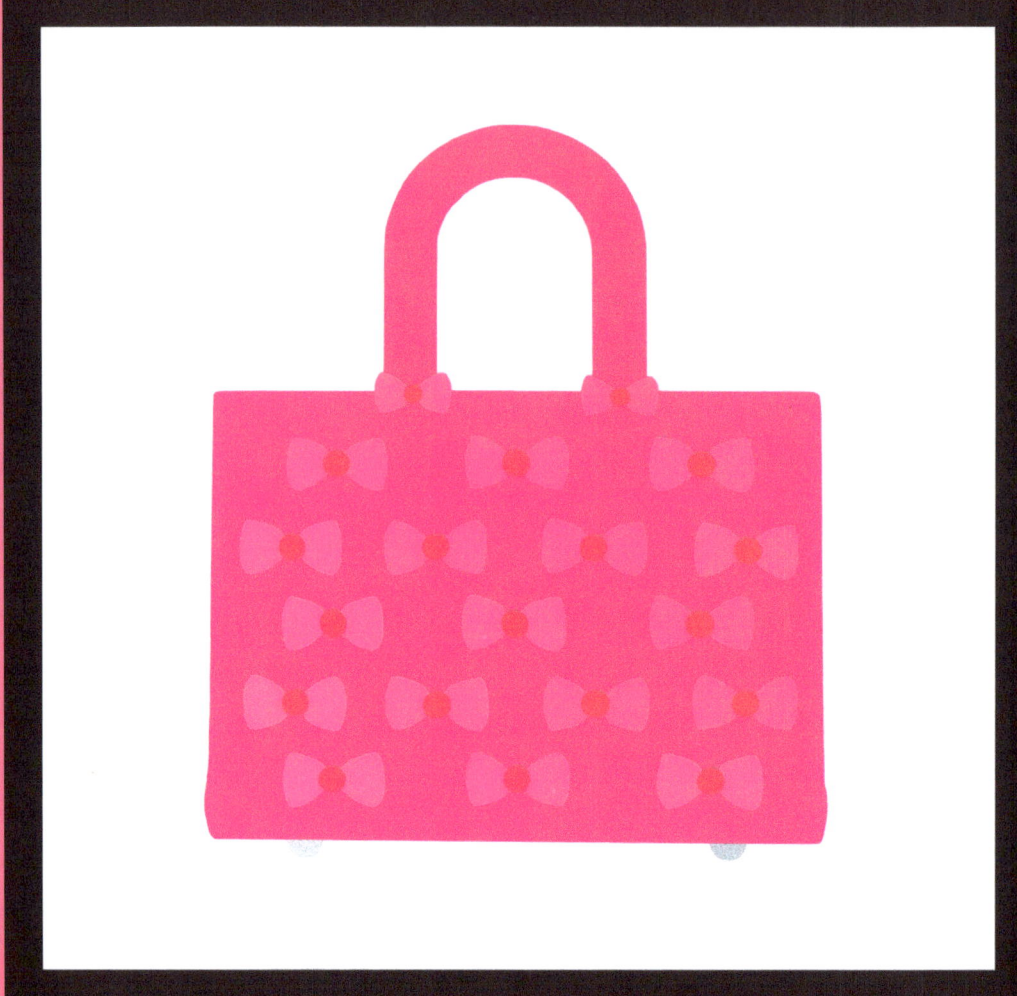

A PINK PURSE IS A FASHION STATEMENT TO WEAR...

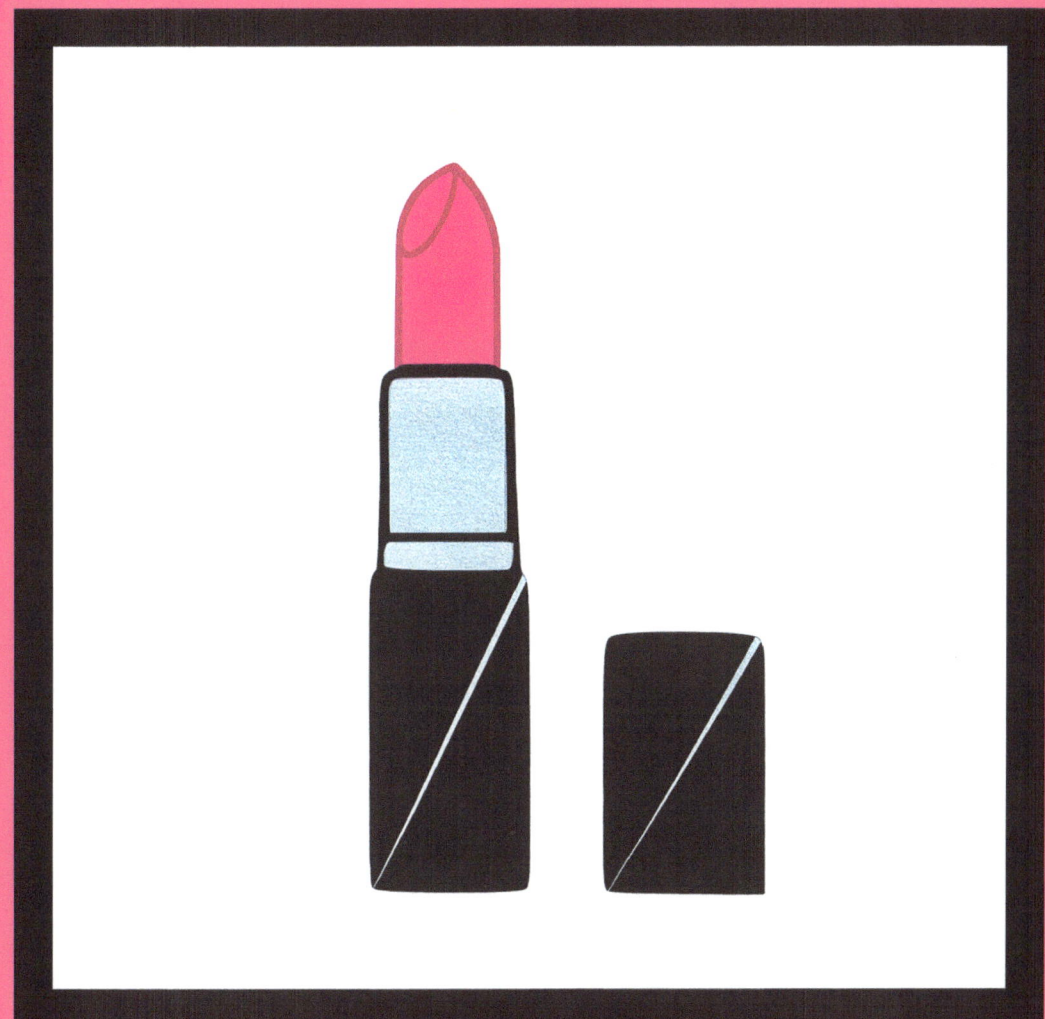

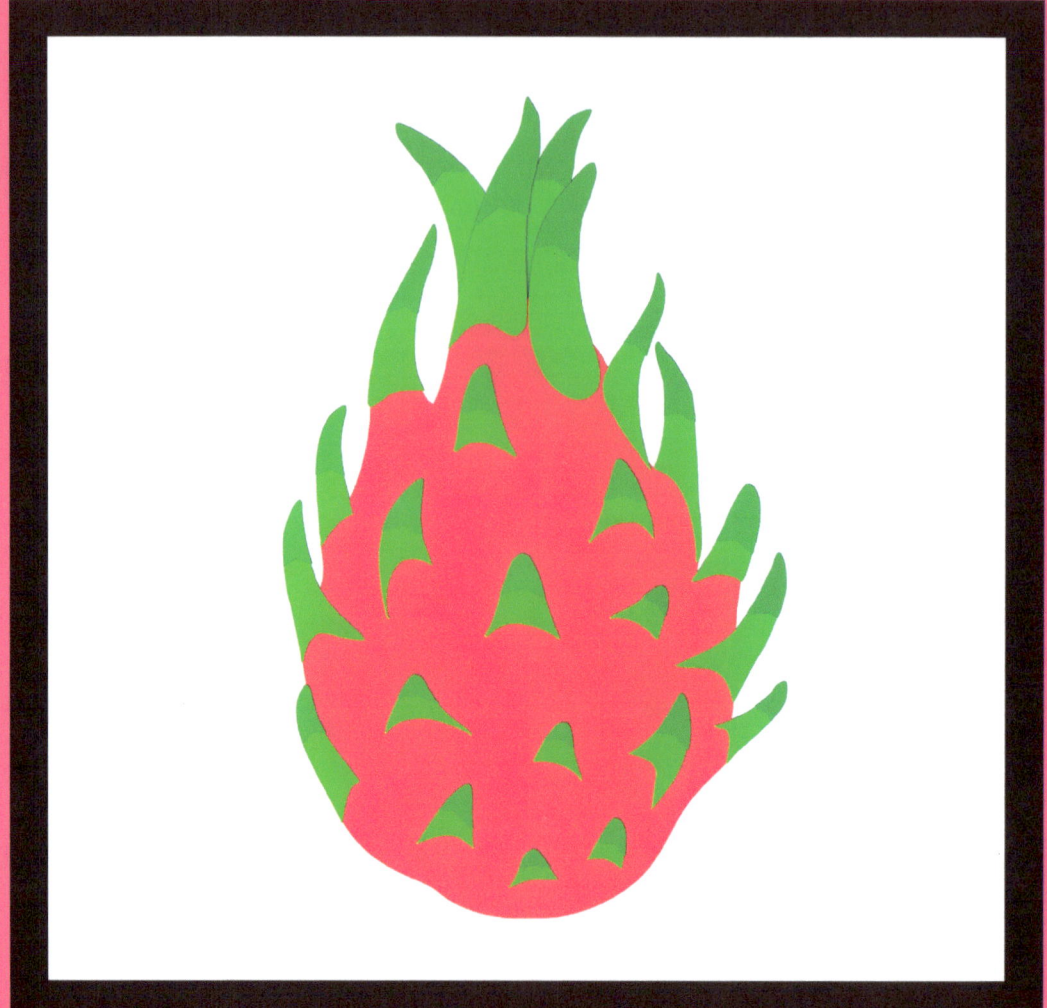

DRAGON FRUIT IS EXOTIC...

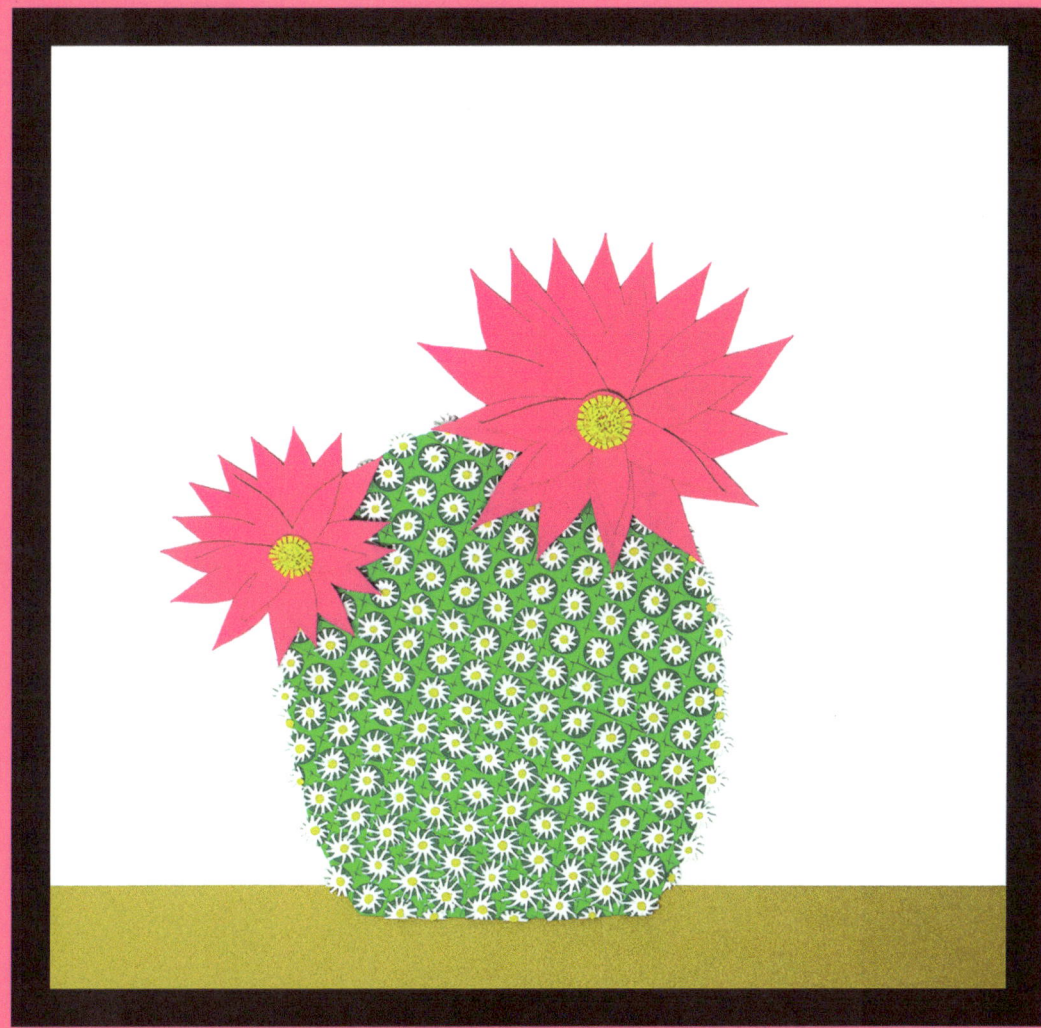

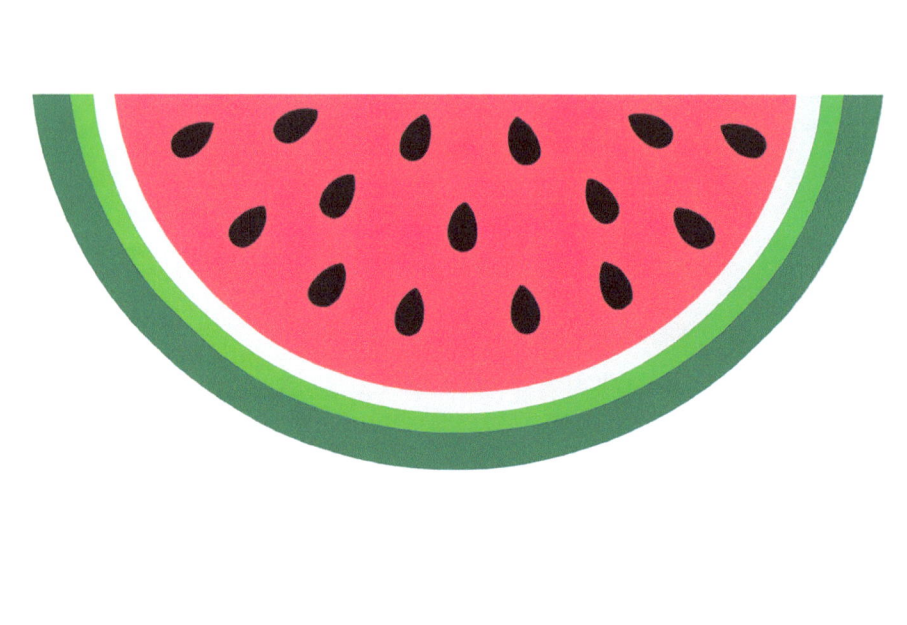

WATERMELON IS A JUICY FRUIT...

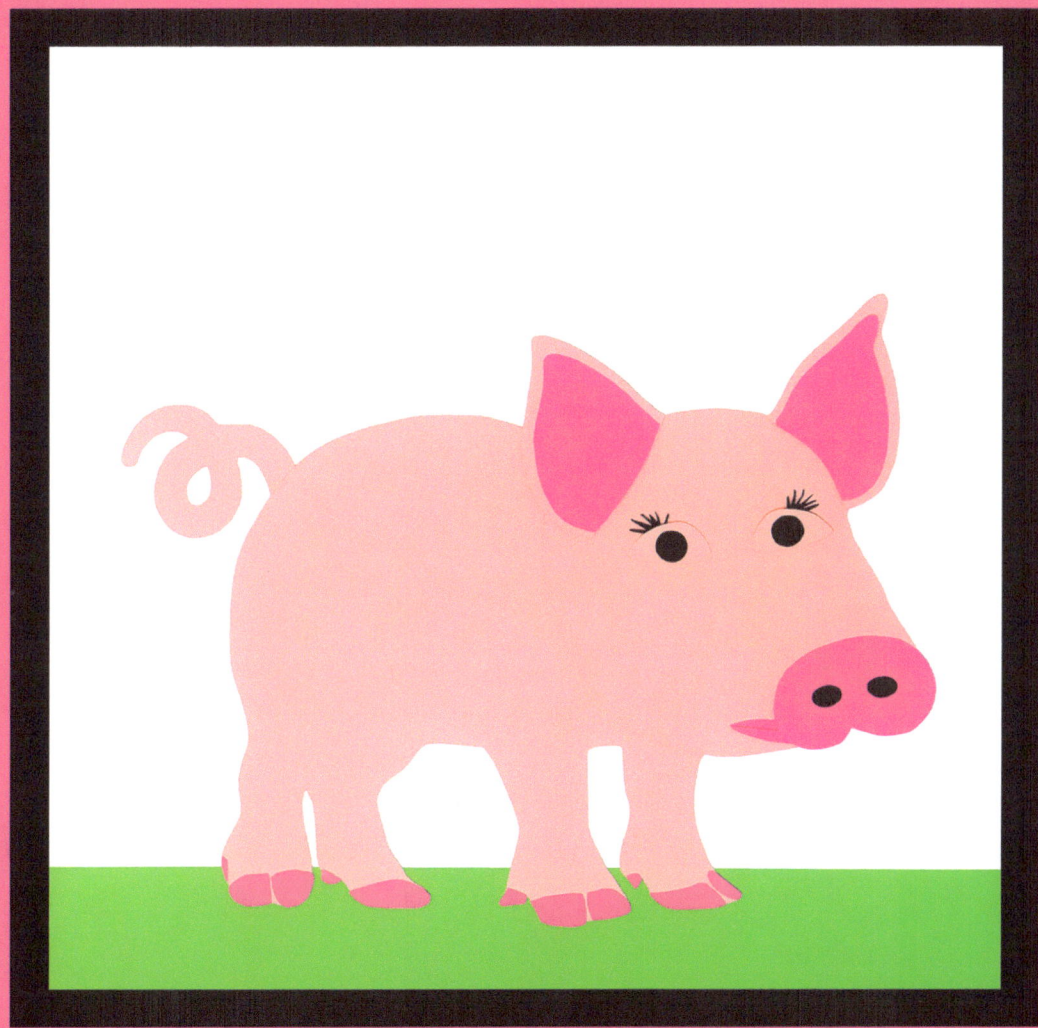

ISN'T THIS PIG EXCESSIVELY CUTE!?

LET'S RE-THINK EVERYTHING WE SAW THAT IS PINK!

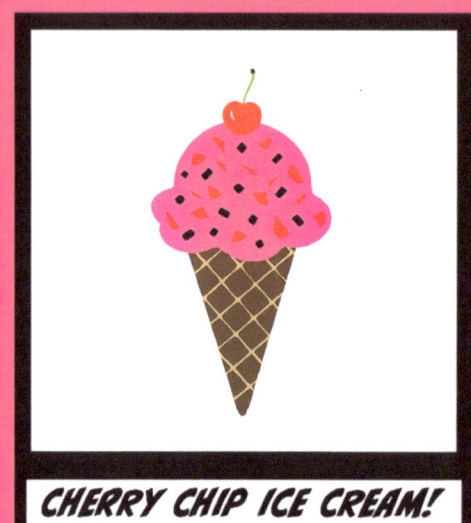

CHERRY CHIP ICE CREAM!

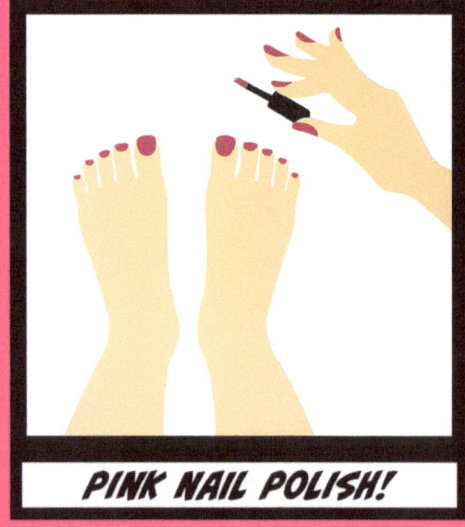

PINK NAIL POLISH!

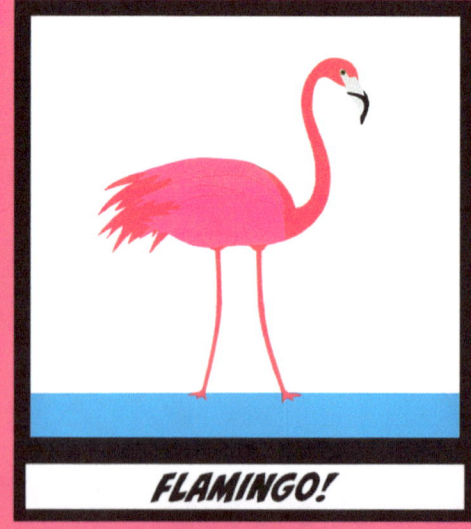

FLAMINGO!

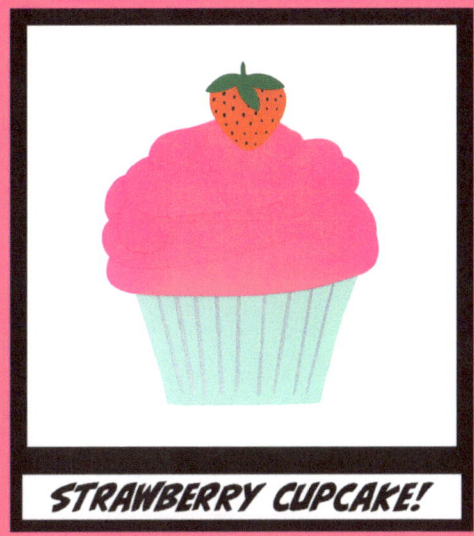
STRAWBERRY CUPCAKE!

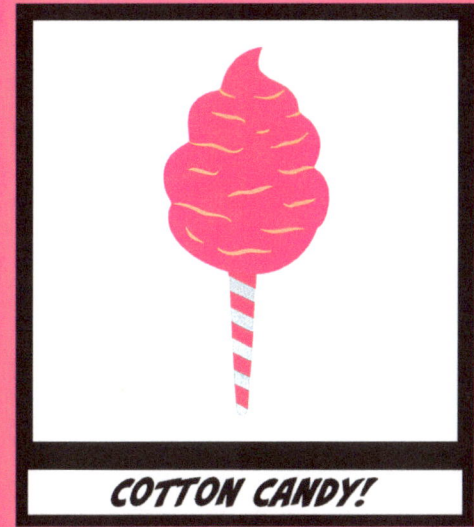
COTTON CANDY!

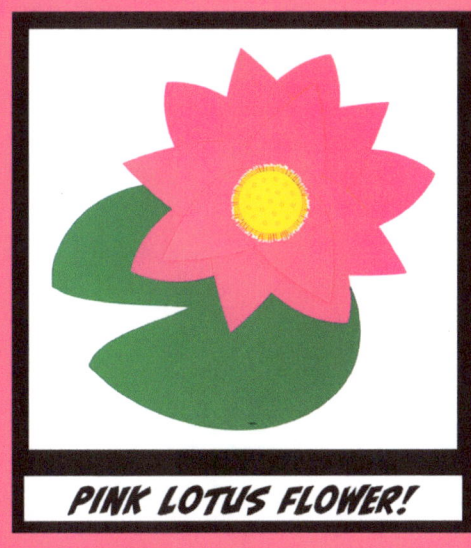
PINK LOTUS FLOWER!

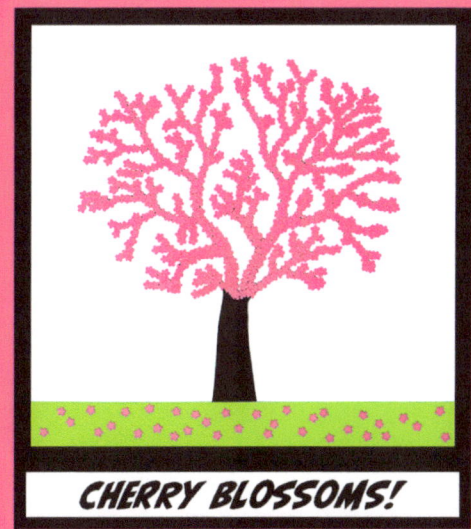
CHERRY BLOSSOMS!

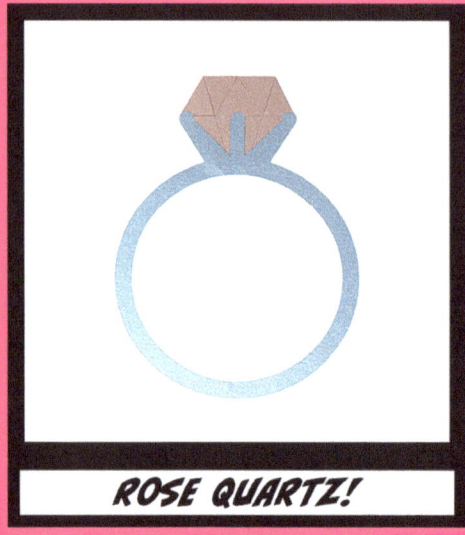
ROSE QUARTZ!

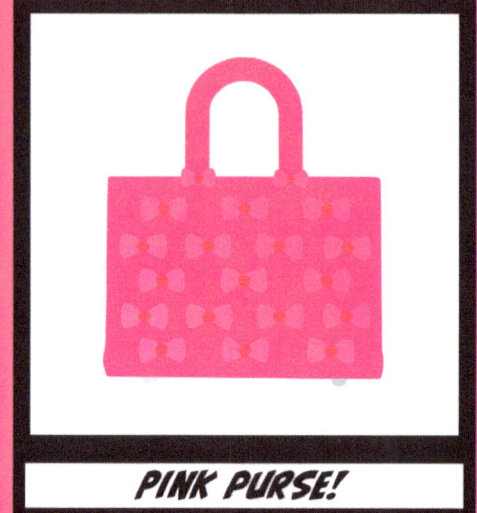
PINK PURSE!

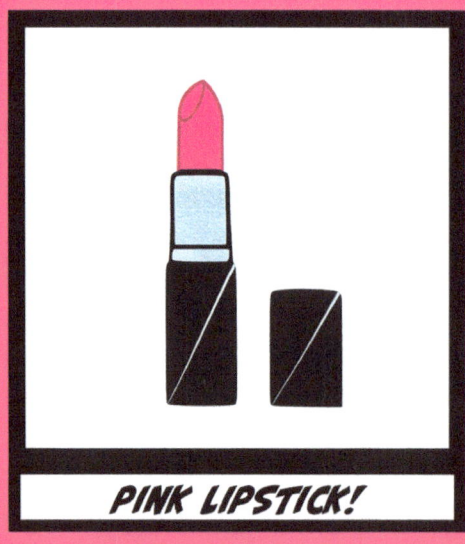
PINK LIPSTICK!

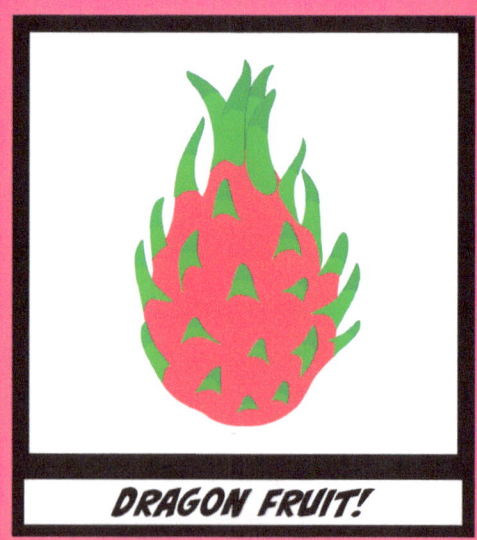
DRAGON FRUIT!

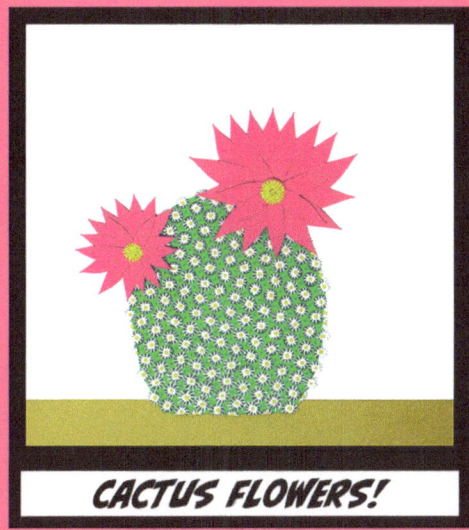
CACTUS FLOWERS!

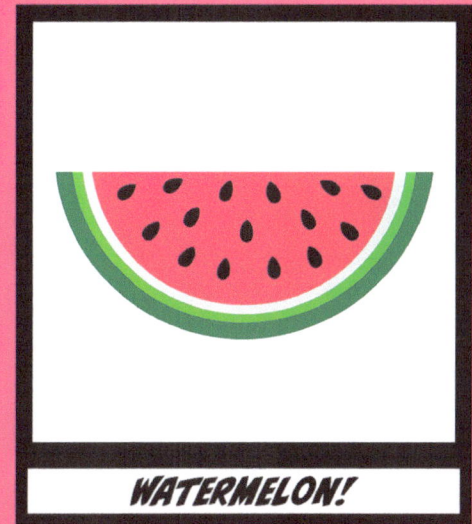
WATERMELON!

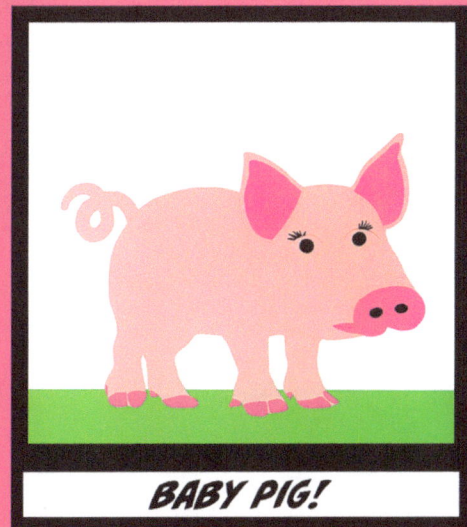
BABY PIG!

NICE JOB, AND NOW WE'RE THROUGH.
ISN'T IT FUN TO LEARN SOMETHING NEW!

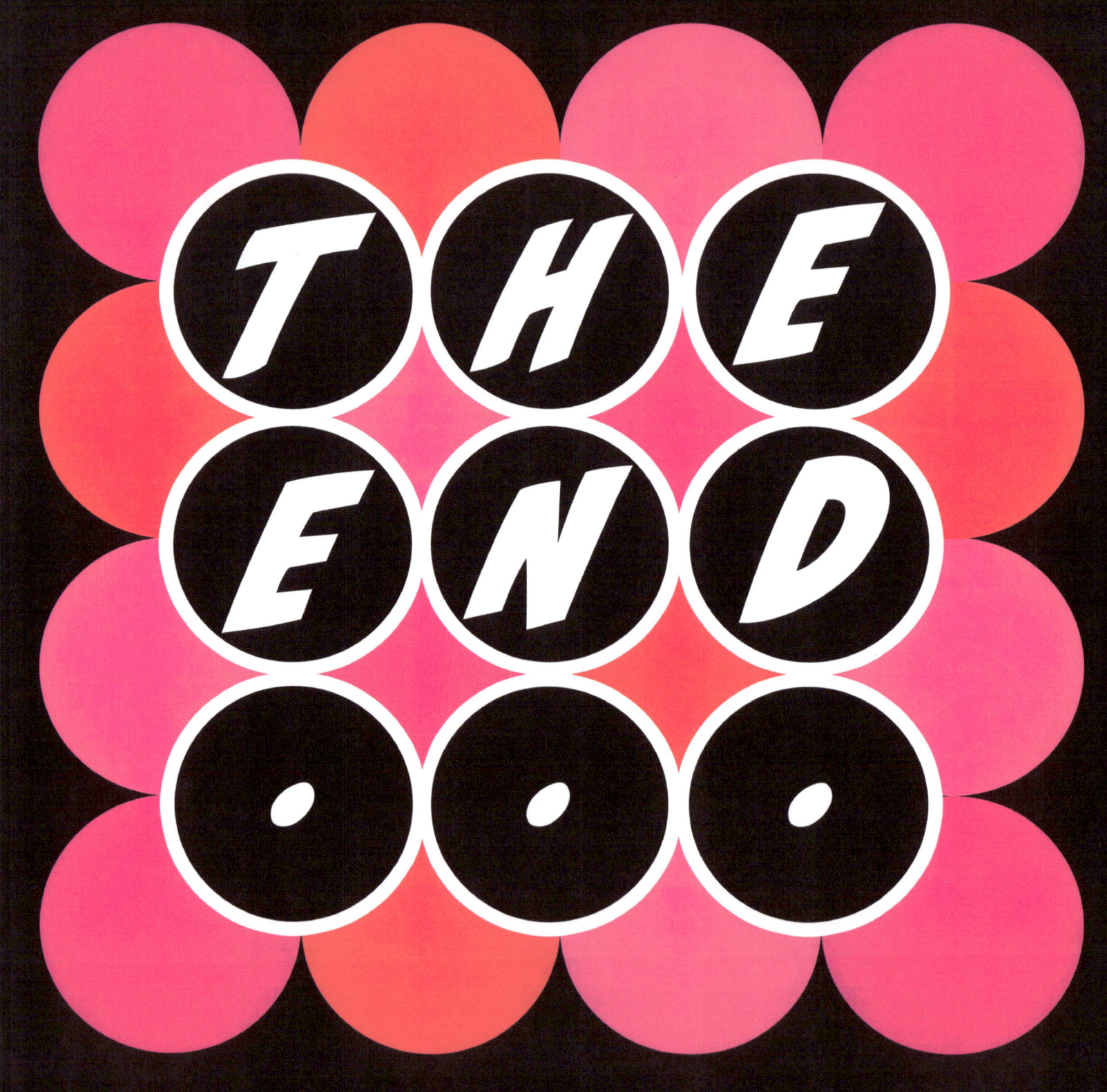

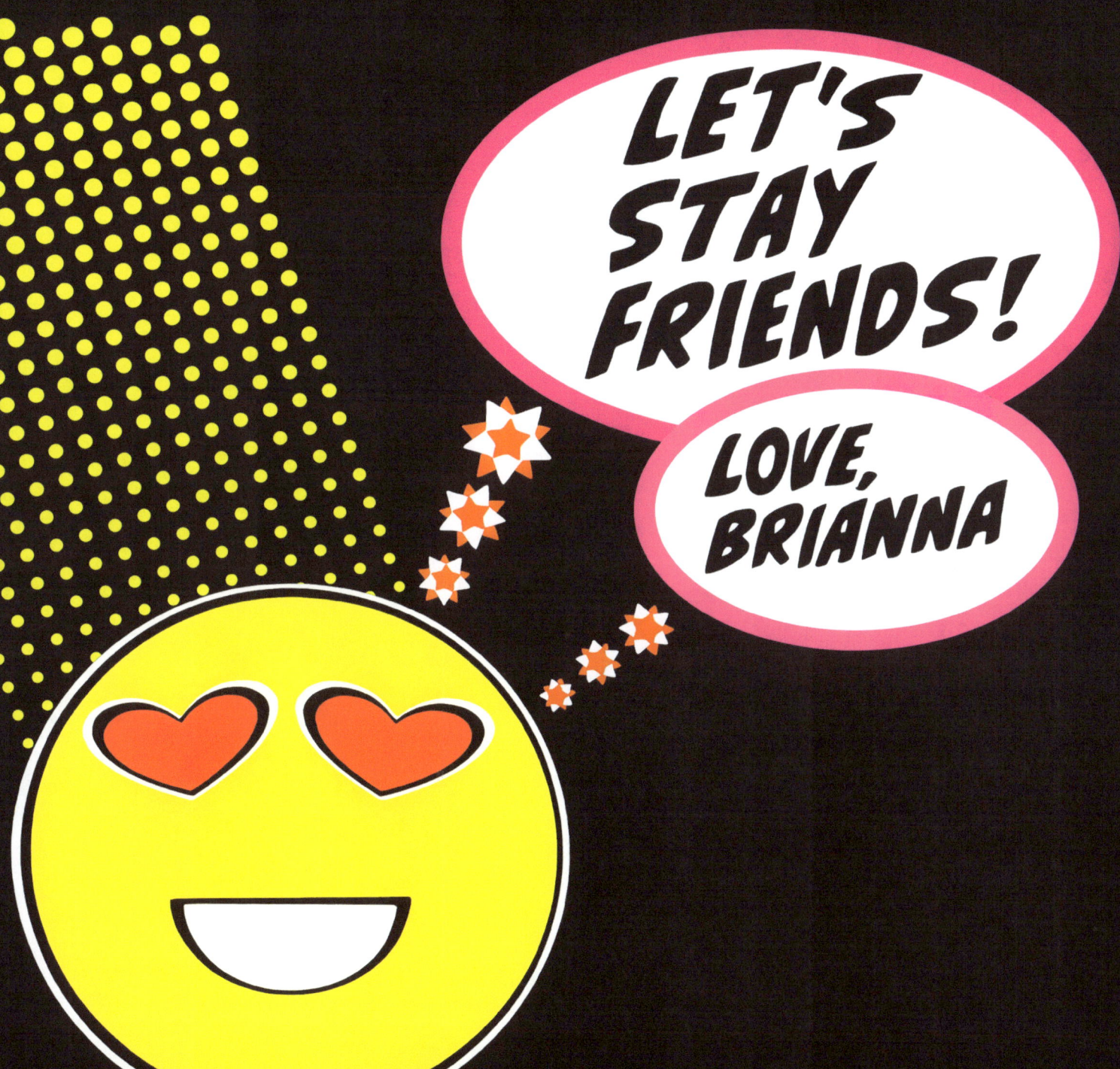

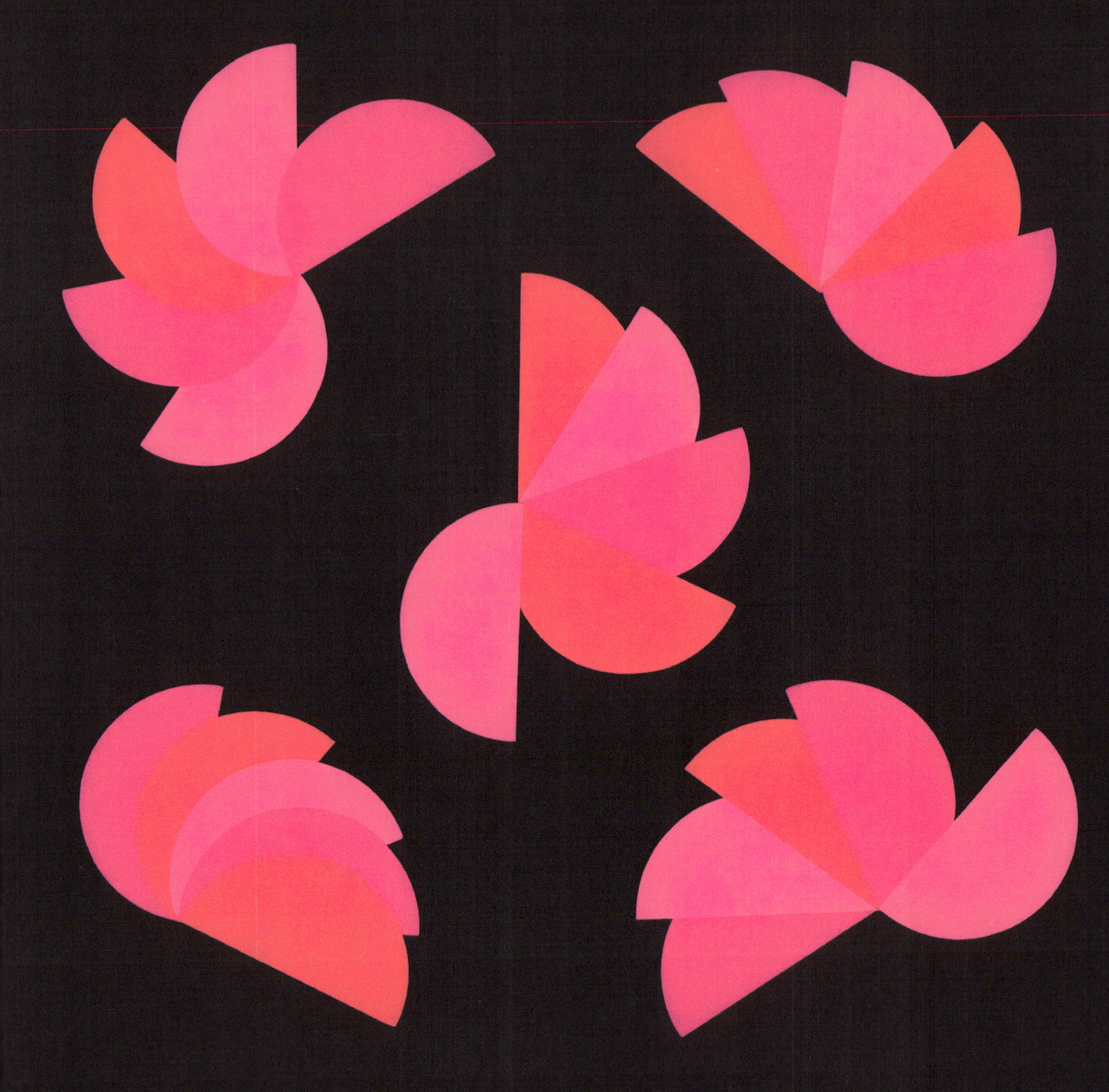

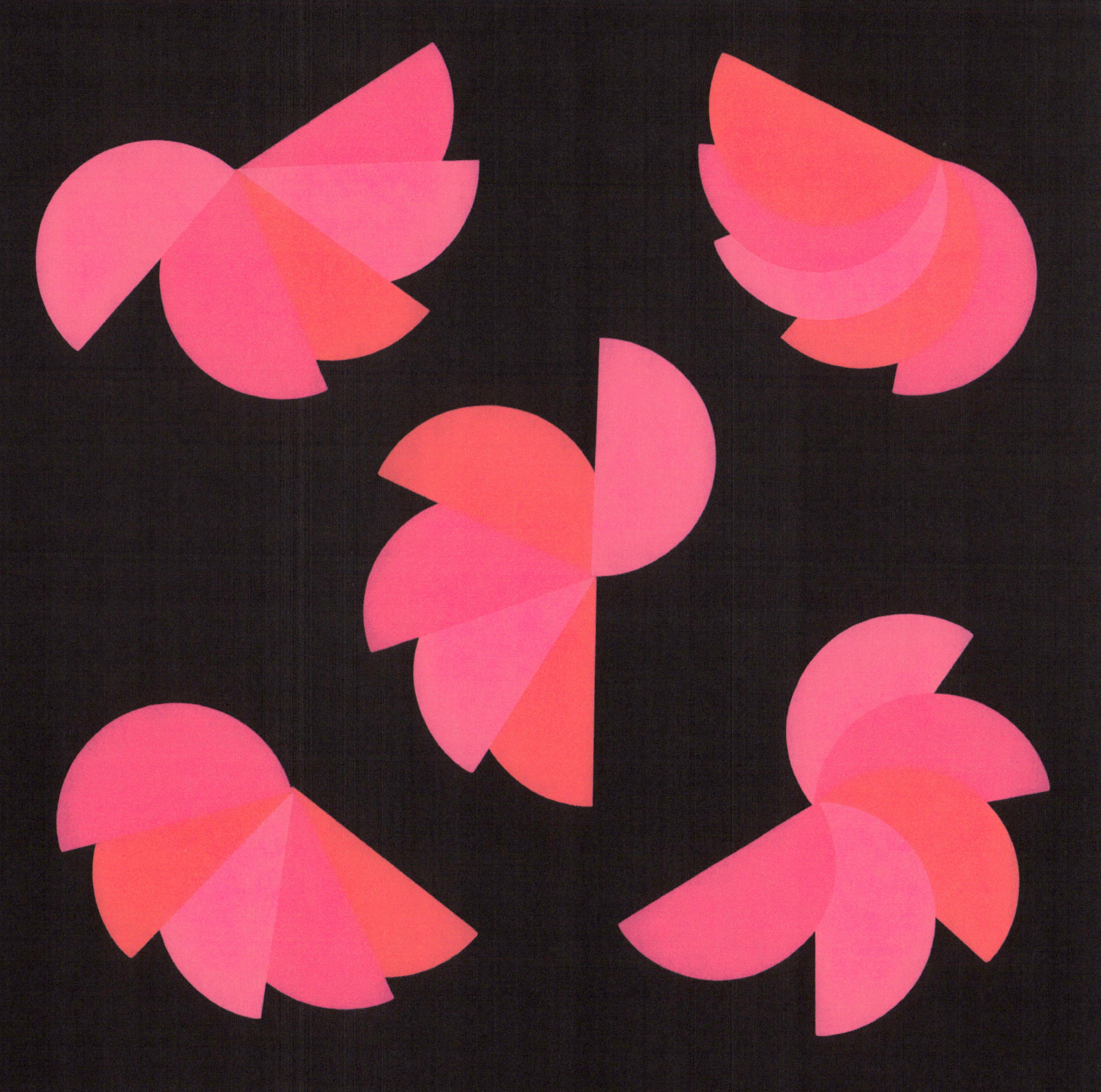

POP ART BOOKs AVAILABLE NOW

- Black and White Night
- Red, I Said!
- Orange Sporange
- Hello Yellow
- Seen Green?
- Blue Hue
- Purple Zurple
- Pop Art ABC's
- Pop Art 123's

Words & Art by: Brianna Davis

www.ingramcontent.com/pod-product-compliance
Lightning Source LLC
Chambersburg PA
CBHW051829210526
45473CB00005B/1805